D0745899

The United States: Historical Atlases of the Growth of a New Nation ™

A HISTORICAL ATLAS OF
North America Before Columbus

Fred Ramen

The Rosen Publishing Group, Inc., New York

For Allison

Published in 2005 by The Rosen Publishing Group, Inc.
29 East 21st Street, New York, NY 10010

Copyright © 2005 by The Rosen Publishing Group, Inc.

First Edition

Library of Congress Cataloging-in-Publication Data

Ramen, Fred.
A historical atlas of North America before Columbus/by Fred Ramen.
    p. cm.—(The United States, historical atlases of the growth of a new nation)
Includes bibliographical references and index.
Contents: Ancient societies of North America—Native tribes of the Pacific Northwest—Native tribes of California, the Plateau, and the Great Basin—Native tribes of the Southwest—Native tribes of the Plains—Native tribes of the Southeast—Native tribes of the Northeast.
ISBN 1-4042-0203-X
1. Indians of North America—Atlases.
I. Title. II. Series
E35.R36 2005
970.004'97—dc22

                                                                              2004041877

Manufactured in the United States of America

On the cover: Top: Sequoyah, the Cherokee scholar and tribal leader who created a written version of the Cherokee language. Bottom: A painting by Karl Bodmer that depicts the Bison Dance of the Mandan Indians.

Contents

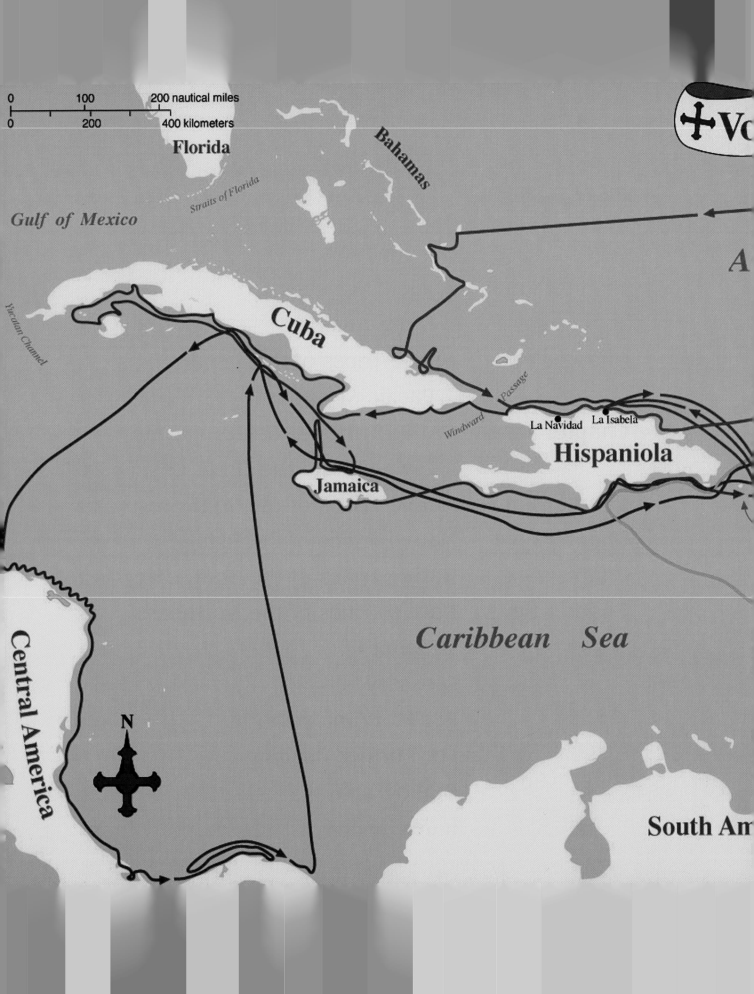

0 100 200 nautical miles

0 200 400 kilometers

Florida

Bahamas

Straits of Florida

Gulf of Mexico

A

Yucatan Channel

Cuba

Windward Passage

La Navidad   La Isabela

Hispaniola

Jamaica

Central America

Caribbean Sea

N

South Am

Vo

✝

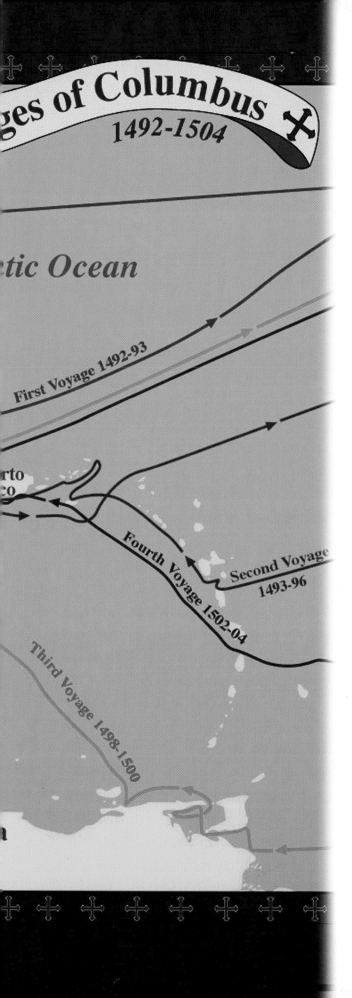

ges of Columbus
1492-1504

tic Ocean

First Voyage 1492-93

rto
co

Fourth Voyage 1502-04

Second Voyage
1493-96

Third Voyage 1498-1500

INTRODUCTION

The day was no different from any other. On a bright morning in autumn, the people of the island awoke as they had done for hundreds of years. In the sleepy villages, dogs played, children cried, and their parents began another day of hard work.

But this particular day, something strange happened. Down on the beach, people could see great white shapes floating over the sea like wings. Never before had they seen such things. Perhaps they were great birds sent by the gods.

After some time, a small boat approached. Inside were men, but very strange men; they were pale, burnt red by the sun in some places. Their faces were hairy, and they wore coverings

This contemporary map illustrates the four voyages of the Italian explorer Christopher Columbus (1451–1506). In 1492, Columbus landed on several islands in the Caribbean (which he believed were located off the coast of Asia). In the 1490s, he made several return voyages to North America. King Ferdinand and Queen Isabella of Spain commissioned Columbus's voyages. In exchange for his discoveries, they agreed to appoint Columbus "Admiral of the Ocean Sea" and viceroy (governor) of the New World.

Although Columbus has been celebrated for his achievements, today he is seen as a controversial figure. Some historians believe that Columbus was a ruthless, greedy man who conquered and enslaved the peoples of the Caribbean. The European arrival in the Americas was devastating to its native peoples. Within a few hundred years, the mixing of cultures brought death to millions of people from disease, warfare, and starvation.

red hats that the islanders eagerly took from them.

The dawn of that morning, October 12, 1492, was truly the dawn of a new era in the history of the world. For the leader of the strangers was Christopher Columbus, an Italian sailor working for King Ferdinand and Queen Isabella of Spain.

Although he was not the first European to ever reach the Americas—the Vikings had reached Newfoundland 400 years earlier—for the first time the native peoples of the Americas came into full contact with Europeans. And despite the friendly nature of their first meeting, the results were disastrous for the Native Americans.

The gentle Tainos (also known as the Arawak), the first native peoples to encounter Columbus, were destroyed within fifty years of the "discovery." Many were ruthlessly enslaved by the Spanish; Columbus himself kidnapped several of them in November 1492 and brought them back to Spain. The

over their entire bodies. They arrived on the beach carrying long knives of shiny metal. The islanders fled back into the forest for a while, but the strangers did little but make strange markings on what looked like white bark. After a while, the islanders left the forest and approached the bearded men. They bowed to the powerful strangers and made signs offering their hospitality. The strangers spoke no language that the islanders understood, but they gave gifts: strange shiny beads and

A rock sits in the middle of this clearing that once served as a ball court in an ancient game played by the Taino peoples. This site is located in present-day Puerto Rico at the Caguana Indian Ceremonial Park. The Taino once thrived in the areas that are now present-day Cuba, the Virgin Islands, and Puerto Rico. Although there is little remaining of what was once a sophisticated culture, a few common English words taken from the Taino language still survive, including canoe, hammock, hurricane, and tobacco.

island of Hispaniola (present-day Haiti and the Dominican Republic), the site of the first Spanish settlement in the Americas, had its population of 1 million people reduced to less than 30,000 in just a few decades. (Some contemporary historians claim that Hispaniola's population was even larger, at least 3 million people or more.)

For the moment, North America, the huge continent Columbus did not even suspect existed, was spared. Its diverse inhabitants continued living much as they had for centuries. But soon their entire way of life would be destroyed. They would be uprooted from their ancestral homes and scattered around the continent.

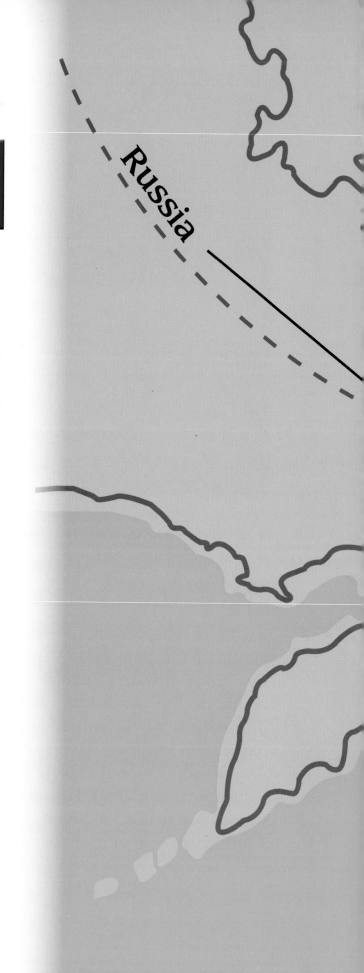

CHAPTER ONE
Ancient Societies of North America

Long before Columbus sailed from Spain toward the west, humans had inhabited the Americas. The precise date of when the first people reached America is not known, but it is at least 12,000 years ago and may be as long ago as 18,000 years.

Earth was in the grips of the Ice Age during that time, a period when the climate was much colder than it is today. Much of Earth's water was concentrated in huge glaciers that covered sections of the Northern Hemisphere.

Because most of the planet's water was frozen, the oceans were shallower than they are today, and sea levels were lower. Accordingly, many areas of the world that are presently under water were dry during this period. One such area is the Bering Strait, a narrow body of water that separates Alaska from Russia. Fifteen thousand

This map shows the probable route of the earliest people to populate the Americas. Approximately 12,000 to 18,000 years ago, Paleo-Indians migrated from Asia to North America across a land bridge made of glacier ice that has since melted. These people made their way south over time and eventually learned to cultivate the land and create sophisticated societies.

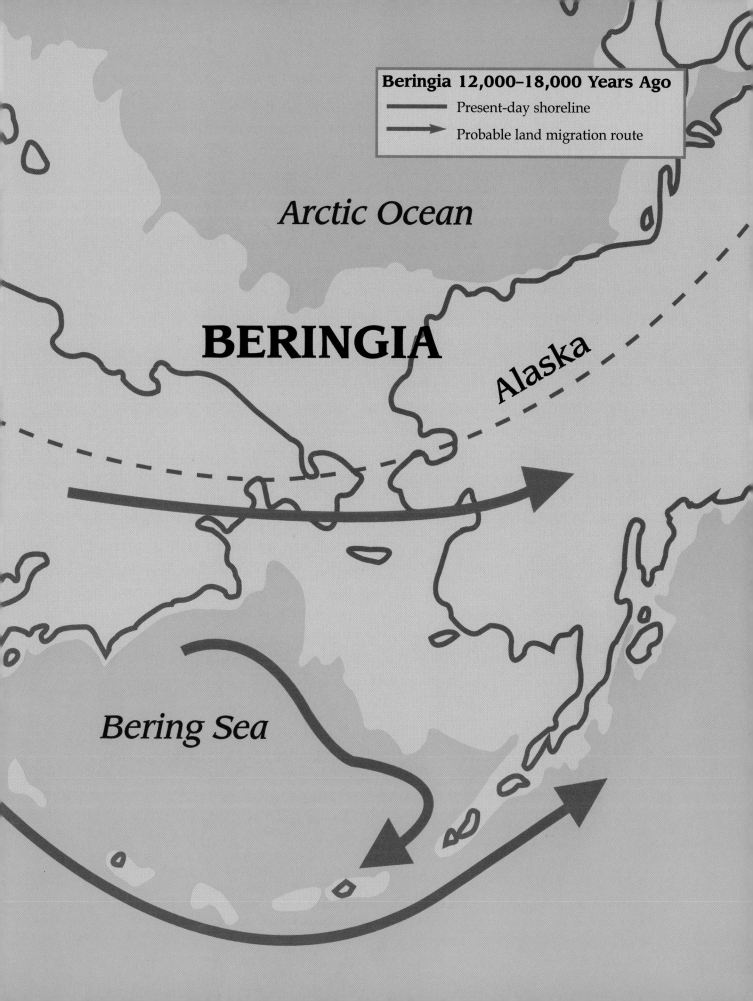

Beringia 12,000–18,000 Years Ago

— Present-day shoreline

→ Probable land migration route

Arctic Ocean

BERINGIA

Alaska

Bering Sea

years ago, however, the bottom of the Bering Strait was above water, creating a natural land bridge between Asia and North America. Scientists call this land bridge Beringia.

It is widely accepted that the first explorers of North America crossed Beringia from Asia. They may have walked, following huge animals like the woolly mammoth, a gigantic relative of the elephant, or they may have crossed in small boats, following the coastline of Beringia. By 12,000 BC, these early inhabitants had established themselves across both North and South America. These people are referred to as the Paleo-Indians and were similar to the Stone Age inhabitants of other parts of the world. They made weapons out of flint and bone, and hunted mammoths and other animals.

Earth was beginning to warm by about 10,000 BC, and the glaciers began to shrink. As the ice melted, humans spread farther into North America. During this time, many animals, including the mammoths, became extinct. Scientists believe that this change was due to the rapidly increasing human population in America. Rising populations may have disrupted the ecology as people hunted many animals into extinction.

As the animals vanished, the Paleo-Indians had to change how they lived. They established settlements, although they still tended to move from place to place several times a year. They also learned to gather more food from plants. In some places, this led to actual farming; however, many groups never became farmers, although all Paleo-Indians ate a variety of plants.

Eventually the people who migrated to the Americas created diverse cultures. Although as many

This flint arrowhead dates from the Neolithic period (New Stone Age). The Neolithic period represents the span of time when stone tools such as this one were first used. During the Neolithic period, settlements appeared around the world because people in many areas were able to go from hunting and food collection to producing the first crops.

as 400 different languages were spoken in North America at the time of Columbus's arrival, all of the Indian civilizations shared the same limitations. For instance, none of them had any beasts of burden, such as cattle or horses. This meant that humans accomplished all the work done by animals in other parts of the world, such as pulling plows or carrying things. Perhaps because of this, none of the peoples of the Americas ever made effective use of the wheel, although some cultures certainly knew of it. Finally, most Indians living in the Americas never stopped using stone and bone to make tools, even when they knew how to work with metals such as gold and silver. For various cultural reasons, these precious metals were reserved for works of art. Even tougher metals such as bronze and iron were never used to make tools or weapons.

The Olmecs

It was in what is now present-day Mexico that the first cities emerged in the Americas. Some 3,500 years ago, a people called the Olmecs emerged in central Mexico. Their culture had many features that strongly influenced other groups across North America. The Olmecs built huge pyramids topped with temples. They had strong leaders and were ruled by chiefs who were both kings and gods. The Olmecs also learned how to farm, specifically a crop known as maize, or corn, which was unknown outside the Americas. This plant continues to be one of the most efficient food crops in the entire world, along with wheat, rice, and potatoes.

Learning how to grow maize was a revolutionary development. This knowledge of farming slowly spread outside the Valley of Mexico, where the Olmecs and their successors, the Toltecs and Aztecs, later thrived. At the time, Toltec and Aztec cities were larger than many European and Asian cities. Many cultures in North America built impressive monuments that still stand today.

The Mound Builders

About 4,000 years ago, in the Ohio River valley, a culture called the Adena began to bury their leaders, along with their possessions, in mounds of earth. Over time, the simple mounds became larger and more complex. For this reason, the Adena and the cultures that followed them are called mound builders. By about 200 BC, the successors of the Adena, the Hopewell people, were constructing enormous mounds, often in the shapes of animals or symbols.

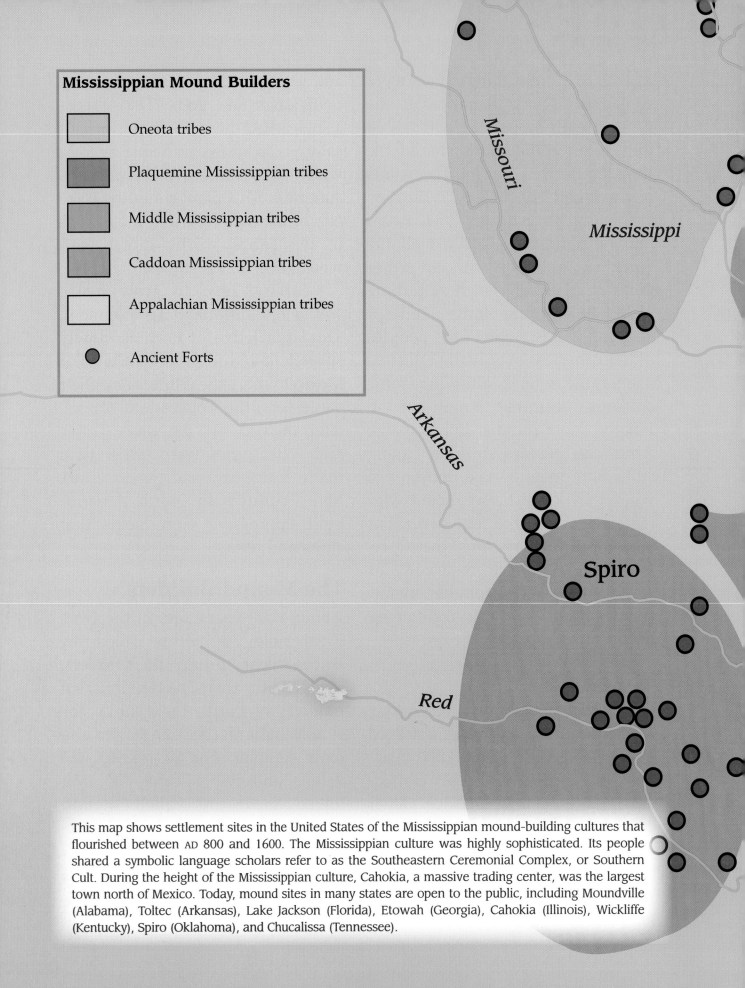

Mississippian Mound Builders

Oneota tribes

Plaquemine Mississippian tribes

Middle Mississippian tribes

Caddoan Mississippian tribes

Appalachian Mississippian tribes

Ancient Forts

Missouri

Mississippi

Arkansas

Spiro

Red

This map shows settlement sites in the United States of the Mississippian mound-building cultures that flourished between AD 800 and 1600. The Mississippian culture was highly sophisticated. Its people shared a symbolic language scholars refer to as the Southeastern Ceremonial Complex, or Southern Cult. During the height of the Mississippian culture, Cahokia, a massive trading center, was the largest town north of Mexico. Today, mound sites in many states are open to the public, including Moundville (Alabama), Toltec (Arkansas), Lake Jackson (Florida), Etowah (Georgia), Cahokia (Illinois), Wickliffe (Kentucky), Spiro (Oklahoma), and Chucalissa (Tennessee).

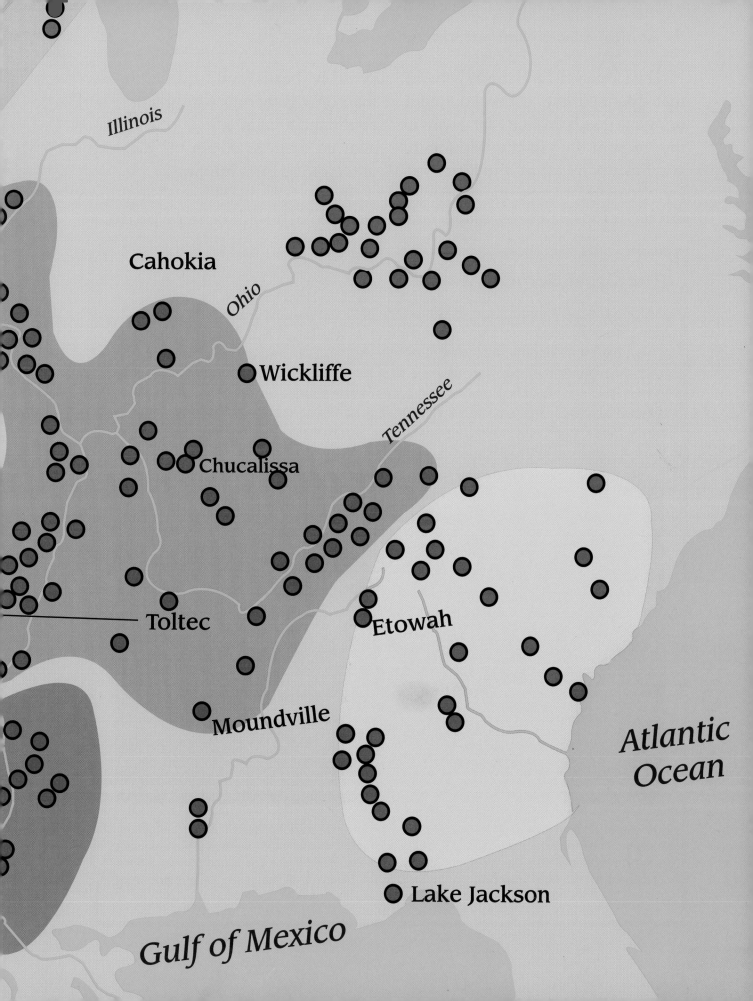

Illinois

Cahokia

Ohio

Wickliffe

Tennessee

Chucalissa

Toltec

Etowah

Moundville

Atlantic
Ocean

Lake Jackson

Gulf of Mexico

The Hopewell had a trade network that spanned the entire continent, bringing goods from as far away as the present-day Rocky Mountains and Florida into the Ohio River valley. In many places, the Hopewell farmed crops such as maize and possibly beans and squash, rather than only gathering wild plants. The abundant animal life of the region allowed them to obtain the majority of their food from hunting.

By AD 500, the Hopewell culture declined. Around the same period, a

The Great Serpent Mound

Among the most famous pictorial mounds is the Great Serpent Mound in Ohio. It depicts a rattlesnake with an oval design at its head, and is more than 1,300 feet (396 meters) in length, 20 to 30 feet (6 to 9 m) in width, and about 4 to 5 feet (1.2 to 2 m) high. Some historians believe that the snake is swallowing an egg while others contend that the large oval is actually the snake's eye. The Great Serpent Mound was likely made between AD 500 and 1200. Other similar mounds depicted birds, bears, deer, and other animals, though many have since been destroyed.

The Great Serpent Mound is similar to other earthworks made by North American mound builders. They are sometimes referred to as effigy mounds, meaning they were made to represent a person or animal. The Great Serpent Mound was discovered in the 1840s and has since been preserved by the Ohio Historical Society. Historians believe that many similar mounds were plowed over when land was settled and farmed throughout the 1900s.

new culture that had ties to both North America and Mexico had begun to develop farther south. These people are known as the Mississippians (800–1600).

The Mississippians inhabited the regions around the Mississippi River valley, including the modern-day states of Arkansas, Alabama, Mississippi, Illinois, and Missouri. Like the Adena and Hopewell peoples, the Mississippians built large earthen mounds. However, few of the Mississippian mounds were burial mounds; instead, they were used as the centers for religious ceremonies. The Mississippian mounds also looked different from those of the Hopewell; they were flat-topped or pyramidal, with sloping sides. Some communities had more than 100 mounds, and some reached heights of 100 feet (30 m).

Like the Hopewell, the Mississippians were farmers who grew maize and beans. Along with their peculiarly shaped mounds, this specific choice in farming indicates that the Mississippians were likely influenced by the cultures of

The Mississippian culture created an abundance of functional, animal-themed art pieces, such as this opossum's head from a bottle that likely carried water. The Mississippians were master craftspeople who used a variety of materials to create both functional and ceremonial art. Works crafted from obsidian, copper, clay, shells, and animal bones were common.

Mexico, who were the first to grow maize and build stone pyramids. The Mississippian society was centered around the value of maize, strong religious beliefs, a common unit of measure, and a sophisticated astronomical system.

The Mississippians were also linked to the cultures of Mexico in the ways in which they structured their society. Each tribe was ruled by a leader called the Great Sun, who was a combination of king, priest, and god. He was a member of a noble class called the Honored Men. The common Mississippians were known as Stinkards. Unlike European societies that had strict rules against class mingling, there was frequent mixing of Mississippians from different classes. In fact, the Great Sun had to have a noble mother and a Stinkard father.

The greatest city of the Mississippians was Cahokia, the City of the Sun, located in present-day Collinsville, Illinois. This city, once home to more than 30,000 people at its height in the 1200s (more population than Paris had at the same time) contained some of the most impressive constructions in America north of Mexico. More than 100 mounds, some rising to a height of almost 100 feet (30 m) once surrounded the city. The tallest of these mounds was known as Monks Mound. Circles of wooden tree trunks called woodhenges have also been found around Cahokia, where Mississippians apparently predicted the change in seasons and other natural events. Cahokia was the center of a far-flung trading network that linked the Great Lakes to the Gulf of Mexico.

This site, located in Collinsville, Illinois, is known as Monks Mound and was once part of the ancient Mississippian town of Cahokia. It is the largest terrace mound north of Mexico and the largest prehistoric earthen construction in the Americas. Scholars believe that Monks Mound was once used for important Mississippian religious ceremonies.

The Mississippian culture began to decline in the 1300s due to internal conflict. Many of its cities were still intact by the time European explorers made their way through the Southeast in the 1500s. Expeditions in this region by the Spaniard Hernando de Soto in the 1540s revealed that some tribes were already dying from infectious diseases, such as smallpox, that were brought to the Americas by the Europeans. Smallpox and conflicts with the Europeans finally destroyed this powerful North American civilization. Within 200 years of de Soto's expedition, the Frenchman René-Robert Cavelier, known as La Salle, noted that some of the same areas (once "very well peopled, with large towns," according to reports written during the de Soto expedition) were completely deserted by 1682.

The Anasazi

In the Southwest, another important civilization had reached its peak in the 1300s, only to vanish from history. This was the mysterious civilization known to us as the Anasazi. The Anasazi were an advanced culture that emerged around 1,300 years ago. They built large pueblos, or flat-roofed masonry structures, in the Four Corners area where Utah, New Mexico, Colorado, and Arizona meet. ("Pueblo" is a Spanish word meaning "town.") Many of their cities had more than 30,000 inhabitants. The Anasazi were farmers and sophisticated astronomers. They built a 400-mile (643 km) network of roads across the rocky desert and canyon floors of the region. The Anasazi lived in relative peace and stability for more than

Cliff Palace in Mesa Verde National Park is one of the best examples of Anasazi aboveground communities. Cliff Palace has as many as 200 separate rooms. Although the structures were protected from outside attack since there were no obvious entrances (the Anasazi entered the dwellings through the ceiling by ladders that were then taken inside), the dwellings were abandoned around AD 1300 possibly due to severe drought conditions and infighting.

1,000 years, but then something terrible happened.

Around 1250, the Anasazi began to leave their settlements, such as present-day Chaco Canyon in New Mexico, and construct towns on the tops of hills. These were places heavily fortified against attack. Then, around 1300, the Anasazi abandoned these dwellings as well and fled south into New Mexico. Why they did so is still a highly debated subject.

It was first believed that the Anasazi departed because of a long and terrible drought, which took place between 1272 and 1299. But they had weathered such droughts before. What has instead become increasingly clear is that the Anasazi turned on themselves. Scholars now believe that a bloody civil war occurred among the Anasazi that ultimately destroyed their entire civilization.

Evidence of horrible massacres has now been uncovered at several Anasazi sites. There is even some evidence of cannibalism during this period. The origin of this violence remains unknown. It was possibly provoked during a civil war or by

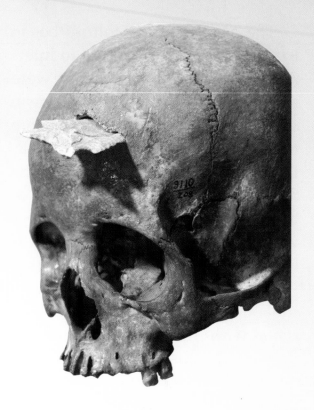

This skull of an Anasazi woman dates to the Pueblo period (AD 700 to 1300). It was discovered with the embedded arrowhead that killed her when she was around twenty years old.

invaders from other regions such as Mexico, which was part of the Anasazi trade network. No matter the source of the decline, the Anasazi society had completely broken down by 1300. The survivors fled south and merged with the Pueblo tribes of present-day New Mexico, leaving behind riddles that may never be answered.

CHAPTER TWO
Native Tribes of the Pacific Northwest

By 1491, the original inhabitants of the Americas had spread out across North and South America and the islands of the Caribbean. Civilizations had risen and fallen, but for most of the millions of inhabitants of North America, life continued as it had for centuries. In each of the regions of the present-day United States—the Northwest, the Southwest, the Great Basin, the Great Plains, the Great Lakes, the Midwest, the Mid-Atlantic, the Northeast, and the Southeast—the cultures had been profoundly shaped by the land's resources.

Land of Abundance

In the Pacific Northwest—the present-day coastal area from southern Alaska through British Columbia and ending near Seattle, Washington—a culture had emerged based around the region's natural bounty. Tribes of the Northwest also produced some of the greatest works of art made by Native Americans.

The Pacific Northwest is a tough and coarse region. Tall mountains fall straight down to the coast and are bisected by powerful rivers and deep valleys. High forests of evergreens grow throughout the region. Because of this rugged landscape, the native peoples of

These petroglyphs (rock carvings) are part of a much larger concentration of designs known as Newspaper Rock, a prehistoric site near Monticello, Utah. The natural dark coating on the rocks, called "desert varnish," provided artists with a way to create figures and patterns by scratching the rock surface with sharp tools.

The reason for this dense population was the area's rich food supply. Along the coast and up the rivers, salmon regularly appear in great numbers, ready to be easily caught. Salmon, large fatty fish whose meat is highly nutritious, are born far upstream in many rivers of the area. Because of the salmon's mating and breeding cycles, huge numbers of fish swim up the rivers of the Northwest six or seven times a year in some places. Salmon were the chief source of food for the Indians of the Northwest. Salmon were caught in nets or traps or were sometimes picked right off the beach. They could be eaten right away, smoked and eaten later, or stored with berries or in cedar boxes filled with oil.

The northwestern Indians captured a variety of sea creatures including whales and seals. They also hunted deer, sheep, and other animals, although these animals were supplemental to the Indians' diet of fish.

The main means of moving around the region was the dugout canoe. This was a long, narrow boat made by cutting down a tree and then using carefully monitored fires to hollow out its interior. Then the rest of the tree was carved into a boat. Some of these canoes were 50 feet (15 m) long and 6 feet (1.8 m) wide.

the Northwest lived along the coast or the riverbanks. Almost all travel was achieved by way of canoe, as the wilderness was too difficult to cross on foot. Farming was totally unknown and probably impossible, given that the native peoples had no animals such as horses or cattle to help clear the land. Yet despite these limitations, the Pacific Northwest may have contained the largest population in the Americas north of Mexico.

Villages in the Northwest were made up of large houses built of wooden planks. At the center of each house was a square sunken area where fires were built. Platforms around this fire pit were used for sitting and sleeping. Each house was inhabited by a large extended

Arts of the Pacific Northwest

Indian tribes of the Pacific Northwest had some of the most talented and productive artists of the Americas. During the long winter months, Indian artisans created beautiful masks, functional objects such as bowls, cups, boxes, and baskets, totem poles, and canoes.

As sculptors, Tlingit, Kwakiutl, and Haida tribes are considered unrivaled. One of the most exquisite and expressive arts of these Northwest tribes is the totem pole, carved from tall red cedar or spruce trees that were plentiful in the region.

Totem poles were meant to act as historical "documents." And while their meaning has been interpreted in many ways, most historians now agree that totem poles recorded the social position of tribal families, often denoting status, class, wealth, and other social facts.

Tribes of the Northwest also often included master metal craftspeople. They often made intricately designed knives, masks, and shields using copper and other available metals.

Tlingit shamans (priests) who magically rescued the soul of a sick person wore "soul catchers" like this one around their necks. The ill person's soul was returned to his or her body after a time in order to make him or her well again.

family, and some houses could be 70 feet (21 m) long. At the front of the house was the totem pole, made up of the heads of animals and spirits carved in wood. Each totem pole was unique to the family who made it.

Common to other world cultures of this period were the religious rituals of northwestern tribes. Spirits were associated with the animals that were hunted and fished. In return for allowing them to catch these animals, the people made offerings to the spirits who guarded them. They believed that failure to do so could cause these spirits to refuse to let the animals be caught, which would lead to the tribes' starvation.

Family structures in this region were unique and complex. In the north, for instance, among the Tlingit, Haida, and Tsimshian tribes, people inherited things from the mother's side of the family. In the central section of the region, however, among the Kwakiutl and Nootka, one could inherit items from either side. In the south, inheritance was specifically from the father's side. Powerful, centralized chiefdoms (hierarchical communities with lords and commoners) only appeared in the southeast, where nobles, commoners, and slaves each had separate roles in society. This structure was in some ways similar to European societies of the same period.

Potlatching

Another remarkable feature of the peoples of the Pacific Northwest was their custom of potlatching, or giving away valuables. A potlatch was a feast; the guests invited were not only fed a large meal but received gifts from the host. Potlatching was done so that the host could move up in society or, more correctly, to show

This Haida mask takes the form of a moon face. Haida members of secret societies often wore masks during ceremonial dances. The Haida commonly made masks and puppets, and both items usually depicted human forms or wild animal spirits, which the Haida called *gagiid*.

Native Americans gather for a potlatch ceremony in this photograph taken in Chilkat, Alaska, in 1895. Unique to tribes of the Pacific Northwest, the potlatch ceremony helped new leaders assert their status in tribal society. During a traditional potlatch ceremony, guests would gather to listen to speeches, eat a grand feast, and receive goods from the person whose status was being revered.

that he already deserved to be considered a higher ranking member. Thus, if a man inherited a good house, he would give generously to his neighbors, showing that he deserved to be considered a more important person. In return for his generosity, his tribesmen would acknowledge their host's higher status.

The tribes of the Northwest were among the most accomplished artists of the period. There were no finer woodworkers anywhere in North America. From the elaborate carvings of their houses to the huge totem poles of their villages, the people of the Pacific Northwest produced amazing works of art, including masks, bowls, and other carved items. They were also accomplished weavers and basket makers. The one medium in which they did not work was clay, so they did not make their own pottery.

Archaeological studies have recently uncovered evidence of iron and steel artifacts in this region that predate the arrival of Europeans. Long before 1492, there is evidence that iron and steel tools, possibly taken from Chinese ships that visited the Pacific coast, were in use. The origin of these tools remains a fascinating mystery.

CHAPTER THREE
Native Tribes of California, the Plateau, and the Great Basin

Dominating the western part of the United States, the Rocky Mountains have had an important effect on the climate of North America. In the Pacific Northwest, they prevent moisture from leaving the coast, resulting in more than 200 days of rain a year. This fertile environment has supported regional tribes for centuries. Farther south, the Rocky Mountains create a vast desertlike region, where there is very little rain. Because of this large mountainous divide, tribes in this region have existed as separate groups.

The Southwest can be divided into three general areas: the Plateau (from Canada south through the eastern half of Washington and Oregon); the Great Basin (Utah, Nevada, and parts of Idaho); and California. Although the cultures of this region were very different,

Until the 1850s, at least 85 different Indian tribes occupied the regions of California, the Plateau, and the Great Basin. All of these various tribes shared some common attributes, including their habits of seed gathering and trading. Because the climates of each region varied, however, each group produced separate and diverse shelters and consumed different diets.

they each relied upon gathering seeds for food and were mostly isolated from other groups.

Native Californians

California had the greatest diversity of tribes, from the Yurok and Hupa in the north, who had been influenced by tribes in the Pacific Northwest, to the southern Mojave and Yuma tribes, who were influenced by the other tribes of the Southwest. (The Yuma grew maize along riverbeds and were the only people in the entire region who farmed the land.) The California region also contained speakers of a larger variety of languages than any other part of North America before the arrival of Columbus.

The Californians survived by gathering acorns and by fishing and hunting small game. Rabbits were an important source of food, and rabbit fur was sewn together to make blankets. Of all the North American tribes, those in California were the best basket weavers. Their baskets were used to gather acorns and other seeds; to carry, store, and transport goods; to capture fish; to support babies; and to trade for other items. Like other tribes of this region, the native Californians were highly independent. Each village existed as a separate unit that might or might not cooperate with members of other tribes.

Indians of the Yuma tribe, once based in and around Arizona, are pictured in this nineteenth-century lithograph. The Yuma were tradesmen who bartered shells from Pacific coast tribes in exchange for baskets and pottery from tribes in the east. They dressed lightly due to the heat in the region, and both men and women commonly painted and tattooed their bodies.

Tribes of the Plateau

The peoples of the Plateau also had some things in common with the tribes of the Pacific Northwest. They caught salmon from the rivers during their traditional runs back to the spawning grounds. The Plateau, however, lacked much of the abundant wildlife found in the Pacific Northwest, and the Plateau tribes, such as the Shuswap and Kutenai, struggled to survive. They gathered seeds and hunted for food. The tribes in the eastern part of the Plateau, such as the Nez Perce and Flatheads, had more in common with the people of the Great Basin than they did with tribes of the Pacific Northwest. The Nez Perce and Flatheads lived in earthen houses but moved from place to place with the seasons.

Tribes of the Great Basin

To the south, in the desertlike region of the Great Basin, the Shoshone, Ute, and Paiute tribes survived in a harsh and forbidding land. (There were hundreds of smaller tribes that also existed throughout the Great Basin; the most well-known include the Washoe, the Kawaiisu, and the Bannock.) Like their northern neighbors, the tribes of the Great Basin fished where they could, although they did not have the advantage of the salmon runs that the tribes of the western Plateau enjoyed. Natives of the Great Basin were far more nomadic than other tribes of western North America. They moved often from place to place, following game animals such as antelope and buffalo. They would herd these animals and smaller creatures such as rabbits into nets or corrals, where the trapped animals could be killed. In the winter, the men of the tribe hunted elk and moose, using snowshoes to get around. Members of the Shoshone, Paiute, and Ute tribes gathered berries and nuts, especially the piñon (pine nut), which was stored through the winter as a source of food. They lived in shelters called wickiups made of tied brush, which were easy to carry when the tribe moved from place to place.

Given the harshness of the areas they lived in, the success of the Plateau, Great Basin, and Californian tribes was remarkable. In a region where they were largely isolated from one another, all managed to thrive despite their limited resources. In the years that followed the arrival of the Europeans in 1492, however, much about their lifestyle changed. Because of long-standing trade relationships between the Great Basin, Plains, Southwest, and Californian tribes, many were influenced by the arrival of the Spanish in the 1540s. The eastern peoples of the Great Basin began using the horse for transportation and migrated to the Plains like many other tribal peoples did after the arrival of the Spanish. In doing so, they adopted many of the attributes of the buffalo-hunting Plains Indians. Soon the Shoshone and Ute tribes, now on horseback, had advantages over neighboring tribes. They began raiding the food stores of other Great Basin peoples such as the Paiute.

The same Spanish invaders who introduced the horse to the Great Basin peoples quickly conquered the California tribes. All across the land, European culture was changing old tribal ways.

CHAPTER FOUR
Native Tribes of the Southwest

The southwestern region of what would later become the United States has long been a civilized region. With its closeness to the great cities of Mexico, this area became the crossing ground of an extensive trade system that tied the ancient cultures of the south with the hunters of the north.

Before about 1300, a thriving and advanced culture known as the Anasazi existed in northern New Mexico and southern Colorado. The Anasazi were most renowned for their amazing buildings, huge complexes of interconnected rooms similar to modern apartment buildings. Yet within 1,000 years, this mighty society had vanished, leaving behind little but empty ruins.

The fall of the Anasazi was not the last chapter in the story of this tough people, however. Their successors, the Pueblo cultures of New Mexico and Arizona, continued many of the traditions of tribes in this region. They built large towns using the same methods the Anasazi had, and they were some of the most successful farmers in all of North America.

The tribes of this region, the Hopi, Zuni, and others, spoke a variety of languages, mostly varieties of Uto-Aztecan including Shoshonean and Tanoan. Each village was independent, and each considered itself the center of

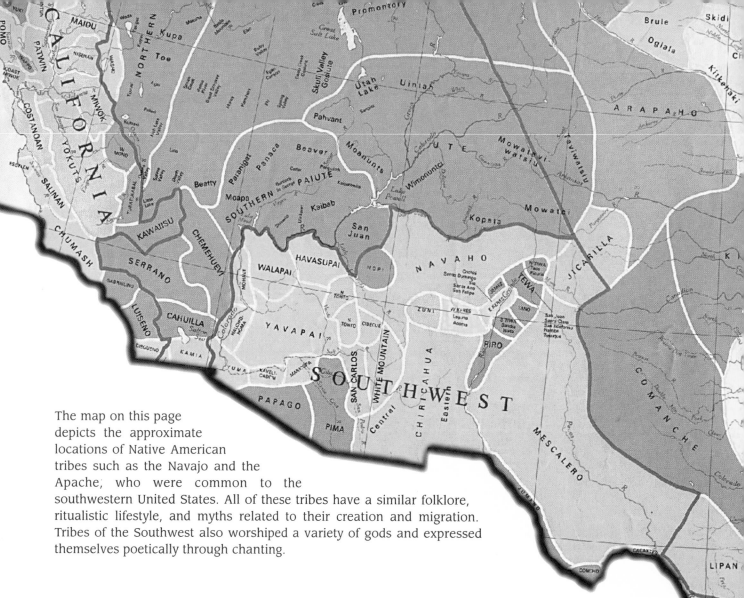

The map on this page depicts the approximate locations of Native American tribes such as the Navajo and the Apache, who were common to the southwestern United States. All of these tribes have a similar folklore, ritualistic lifestyle, and myths related to their creation and migration. Tribes of the Southwest also worshiped a variety of gods and expressed themselves poetically through chanting.

the universe. The towns were small, most never having more than 3,000 inhabitants. There was great variety in the design of each town, but all of them shared common elements such as the materials used in their pueblo structures.

The most important concern for each village was maintaining its crops. The Pueblo tribes were expert farmers, even in the limited climate and harsh conditions of the hot desert. Their most important crop was maize, but they grew it along with beans and squash, harvesting large amounts of food. Men did most of the farming and they also hunted small game, while women artisans created pottery. The pottery of the Pueblo tribes is regarded as some of the finest produced by Native Americans. Both Pueblo men and women wove cloth in elaborate patterns.

Religion was the center of Pueblo life. Rituals were an important part of each day, especially rites related to praying for rain. Ceremonial dances and songs were performed to celebrate the seasons and to pray for good fortune throughout the year. Some of these ceremonies lasted as long as a week and involved costumes and figural masks. Among the Hopi, small dolls called kachinas were also an important part of religious life. Each doll, carved from the roots of the cottonwood tree, represented a different god or spirit. The men of the villages joined kachina societies and dressed up as the different kachinas during rituals and dances.

Great secrecy was attached to Pueblo rituals. Each village had its own interpretation of the rites to be followed. The men who performed the ceremonies were members of secret societies that only slowly revealed their rituals to the younger men of the tribe.

In addition, Pueblo societies that controlled hunting, public order, and trade were "clown" societies, whose members ridiculed anyone who did not strictly follow the Pueblo ideals of modesty and cooperation. Pueblo society emphasized the importance of the tribal unit over that of the individual member. This idea was somewhat unique in Native American culture. Being a productive member of a tribe and working to help the village survive were among the most important aspects of Pueblo life.

The Hopi and other tribes of the Southwest created kachina dolls as religious and teaching tools. Each doll represented the spirit of an animal, plant, or human. This Hopi kachina is on display at the Heard Museum in Phoenix, Arizona.

Pueblo villages were made of stone or adobe, which is a mixture of mud and straw that dries hard in the sun. Stone buildings were often plastered over with clay. These stone or adobe structures were entered through trapdoors in the roof; ladders led down from the roof to the ground. Each family had at least two rooms in a structure. Buildings were often expanded as the family grew, and rooms were sometimes built

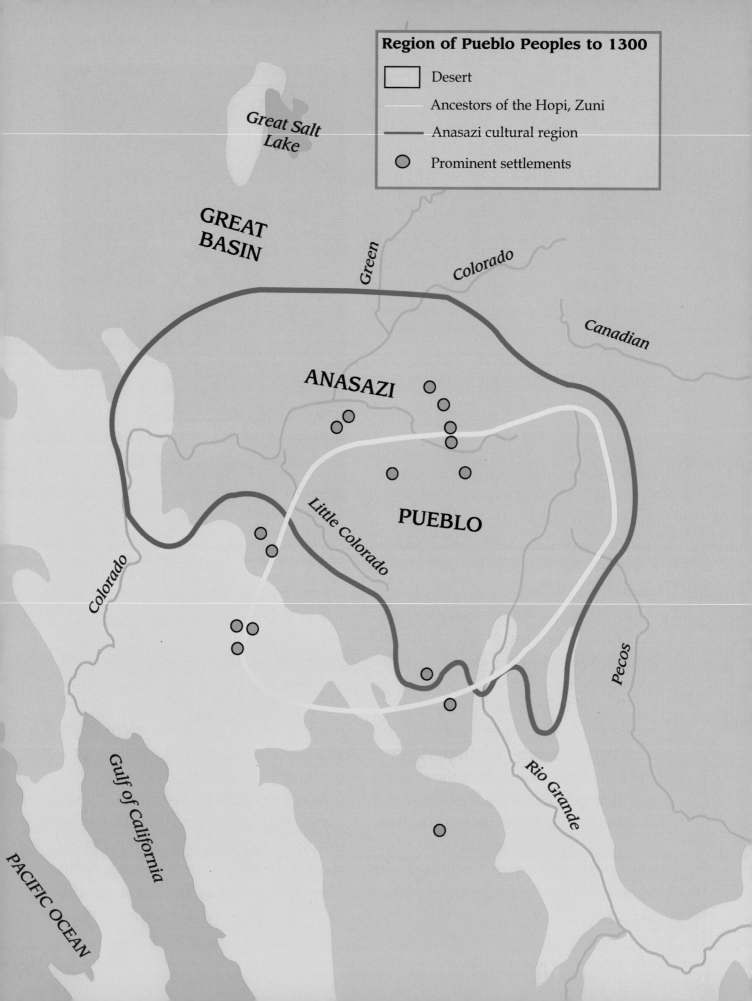

Region of Pueblo Peoples to 1300

◻ Desert

Ancestors of the Hopi, Zuni

Anasazi cultural region

◯ Prominent settlements

Great Salt Lake

GREAT BASIN

Green

Colorado

Canadian

ANASAZI

PUEBLO

Little Colorado

Colorado

Pecos

Gulf of California

Rio Grande

PACIFIC OCEAN

directly on top of each other. Underground rooms in each structure, often used for storing food, were called kivas. Only men were allowed into the kivas, where they sometimes discussed tribal issues or performed sacred rituals.

The Navajo and the Apache

The Pueblo were not the only residents of the Southwest at the time of Columbus's arrival in the New World. The Navajo and the Apache had migrated into the area during the 1400s from the north as far as Alaska, and both spoke Athabaskan languages.

The Navajo (who called themselves Dineh, a word meaning "the people") were originally nomads. The Pueblo considered them a warrior tribe, because the Navajo often raided Pueblo kivas. Over time, Navajo tribes settled. They adopted aspects of Pueblo culture into their own lifestyle, becoming accomplished weavers whose blankets and other woven items were highly sought after. They lived in eight-sided houses of wood covered with bark and earth called hogans. After the coming of the Spanish in the sixteenth century, Navajo tribes became sheepherders. Today the Navajo are the largest tribe in the United States, with more than 180,000 members.

The Apache, a Zuni word meaning "enemy," actually called themselves Inde, or "the people." Like the Navajo tribes, the Apache were nomadic warriors. They migrated west and gradually settled. However, not all Apache tribes adopted this settled lifestyle; some continued to raid the Pueblo, stealing their food and animals. Few peoples have been as hardy as the Apache or matched their ability to survive in an unforgiving landscape.

The great period of Apache history began after contact with the Spanish. Once the Apache acquired horses, they became masters of a rugged expanse of the Southwest and northern Mexico. Within a few years, the mere mention of the Apache terrified Spanish, Mexican, and American settlers. The Apache dominated the Southwest for centuries until the Americans finally conquered them in the 1800s.

This map illustrates the concentration of Pueblo peoples, including the Anasazi, and their major areas of settlement to 1300. The name Pueblo was derived from the small cliffside dwellings. All Pueblo Indians share similar rituals, languages, religious practices, government, and customs.

CHAPTER FIVE
Native Tribes of the Plains

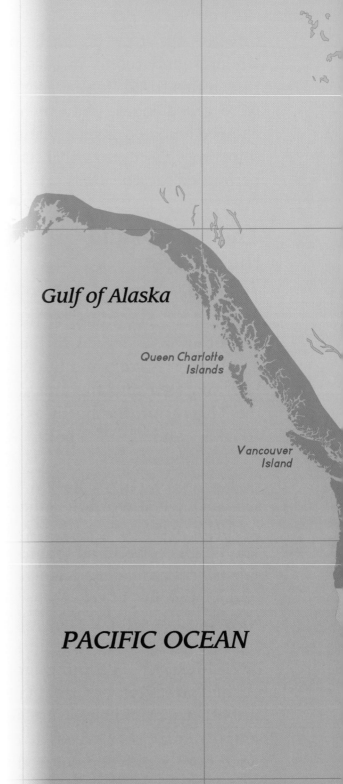

Gulf of Alaska

Queen Charlotte
Islands

Vancouver
Island

PACIFIC OCEAN

The native peoples of the North American Plains—the flat grasslands from the Appalachian Mountains in the east to the Rocky Mountains in the west—are among the most well-known Indian cultures. Many of the common characteristics associated with Native American culture, from the feathered headdresses called war bonnets, to the tepees made of buffalo hide, originated with Plains Indians.

Before the arrival of the Europeans, the Plains Indians could be categorized into two groups: those tribes who planted seeds and harvested crops for their food, and those who survived mostly by hunting animals. The farming tribes remained the larger and more powerful group of the two until cultural changes caused by later contact with Europeans disrupted their control over the region.

This map of North America illustrates the approximate locations of Native American tribes and their settlements around 1500. Since the migration across Beringia thousands of years earlier, native peoples have spread from the Plains to California and the Southwest and then east, moving into the woodlands of the North Atlantic. Around 1500, more than 200 languages and dialects were spoken by various tribes.

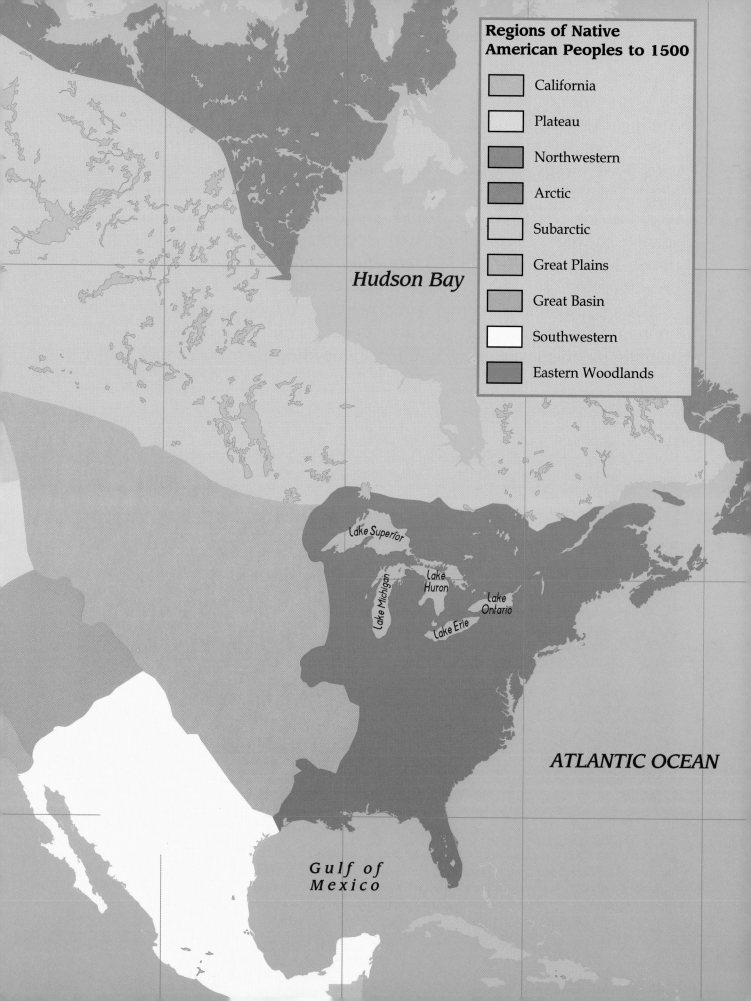

Regions of Native American Peoples to 1500

- California
- Plateau
- Northwestern
- Arctic
- Subarctic
- Great Plains
- Great Basin
- Southwestern
- Eastern Woodlands

Hudson Bay

Lake Superior

Lake Michigan

Lake Huron

Lake Erie

Lake Ontario

ATLANTIC OCEAN

Gulf of Mexico

The Mandan

Among the largest tribes on the Plains were the Mandan, a group who lived mostly in what is now North Dakota. The Mandan women were farmers who grew maize and squash in the valleys along the upper Missouri River while men grew tobacco.

Young Mandan men were hunters. One of the most difficult animals for them to hunt was the buffalo. Because they did not have horses, all hunting had to be done on foot. This was very dangerous because the Mandan did not have any means of quick escape if the kill somehow went awry and the animal retaliated. The Mandan worked together to hunt these mighty buffalo, some weighing more than 2,000 pounds (907 kilograms). They would gather and herd them toward a cliff or a fenced-in corral, stampeding them until they either

Mandan Indians perform a buffalo dance in this nineteenth-century oil painting by Swiss artist Karl Bodmer. At the time, Mandan Indians were entitled to join various different societies, each based on the age of its members. Symbols from each society were shown in the dress and weaponry of each tribal member. The most highly regarded society of the Mandan was the buffalo bull society, since buffalo were so difficult to capture.

plunged over the cliff or were trapped inside the fence and therefore easier to kill. Buffalo provided food, clothing, shelter (made from their thick hides), and tools (made from their bones and horns).

The Mandan had two kinds of houses: one with a roof of hide supported by poles, and another made up of a framework of cottonwood or willow branches covered by earth. They lived in settled villages and traveled only to hunt.

Religion played an important part in the lives of the Mandan. Like many of the other Indians of North America, they believed that everything around them had its own spirit, which had to be respected or it might try to harm them. One of the most important Mandan ceremonies was the Okeepa festival, which occurred in midsummer. During the Okeepa, the young men of the village performed the Sun Dance, a ritual shared by many of

The central pillars and roof beams of this Mandan hut are clearly visible in this nineteenth-century oil painting by Karl Bodmer. During the winter of 1833 to 1834, Bodmer painted a number of portraits of the Mandan, which were later published in a book called *Bodmer's America*. Permanent Mandan huts were typically about 35 feet (11 m) in diameter.

the Plains cultures. During the Sun Dance, men punctured their skin on their legs, chests, backs, and arms with knives. Wooden sticks were slipped through these cuts, and leather thongs tied to the sticks; the men were then hoisted into the air by these thongs. Although the pain brought on by these actions was incredibly intense, the Mandan struggled not to pass out. This ritual was a way to prove a man's bravery and courage. The scars that remained from the Sun Dance were considered marks of honor.

Men were also the warriors of the Mandan. War represented both ritual and conflict for many of the Plains tribes; sometimes, killing an enemy was not as important as having demonstrated bravery during a battle. One common feature of Mandan warfare was counting coup—by touching an enemy, either living or dead, a man could increase his honor. Rules carefully governed who could count coup against an enemy and how often.

Medicine Wheels

One enduring mystery from the Plains region is the medicine wheel. Scattered throughout the northern Plains region—Wyoming, Montana, and southern Canada—are large rings made up of rocks laid on the ground. Most medicine

The Mandan, a relative of the Sioux, were revered for their peaceful nature and farming talents. Mandan Indians were able to produce a hybrid breed of maize, which was able to grow well with less rainfall, one of the reasons why they were a settled and peaceful culture. This portrait of a Mandan Indian was created by Edward S. Curtis and published in a book about the Mandan in 1909.

wheels are identified by one or more concentric stone circles and one or more lines running outward from their center. Another type of medicine wheel often had a pile of stones at the center. Sometimes these sites were used as burial grounds, proven by the human bones that have been found in them. The wheels are sometimes quite large, ranging from 30 to 100

This Native American medicine wheel sits atop Medicine Mountain in Bighorn National Forest near Sheridan, Wyoming, and was the first Native American construction known by the term. Medicine wheels often share a concentric circular design with lines that radiate from their center. To this day, scholars don't know why the medicine wheels were constructed.

feet (9 to 30 m) in diameter. Little is known about why the wheels were made or who built them. They may have served as a kind of astronomical observatory, like England's Stonehenge, or possibly been used as calendars.

During the time just before Columbus's arrival, other tribes were moving into the Plains region, including the Kiowa and Absaroka (who are also known as the Crow). These Indians were generally nomadic and relied on hunting rather than farming. It was these groups, along with later immigrants like the Lakota and Cheyenne, that would later become famous tribes of the Plains. They adopted the horse into their culture after the arrival of the Europeans and became great hunters and warriors. For the farming tribes of the Plains, the Mandan and Hidatsa, the Omaha and the Wichita, the future was less certain. Within a few years after the arrival of the Europeans, disease and invasion largely destroyed them.

Some of North America's strongest societies carved a plentiful existence out of the dense forests east of the Mississippi River. In the Southeast, ancient Mississippian chiefdoms once governed mighty cities. Even in its decline, the Mississippian civilization was a strong cultural influence on the regional cultures that later emerged.

Although Cahokia, its greatest city, had been abandoned, other important outposts of the Mississippian tradition were thriving. One was Natchez, in the present-day state of Mississippi. Like the Mississippians, the people of Natchez were influenced by the civilizations of Mexico. They worshiped the sun as their primary god and sacrificed human beings to it. They had a strong, centralized government. Their ruler was considered the brother of the sun and a god in his own right.

This hand-colored map, housed in the U.S. Library of Congress and created by Albert Gallatin, illustrates the locations of Indian tribes of North America around 1600. The tribes are divided into eleven linguistic families. The map was originally published in 1836 by the American Antiquarian Society.

Eskimaux	Blue.
Athapascas	Red.
Algonkin-Lenape	Yellow.
Iroquois	Brown.
Cherokees	Purple.
Creeks	Red.
Choctas & Chicasas	Red.
Sioux	Green.
Black Feet	Purple.
Pawnees	Yellow.

MAP
of the
Indian Tribes
of
NORTH AMERICA
about 1600 A.D.
along the Atlantic;
& about 1800 A.D.
westwardly.

Published by the Amer: Antiq: Soc:
From a drawing by Hon: A. Gallatin.

Pendleton's Lithography.

Natchez and other cities dotted the Southeast at the time of Columbus's arrival. Although they were still there when French explorers came through the area in the early 1500s, European disease and warfare had nearly eliminated their society; later explorers of the Southeast found almost no trace of the great cities that had existed just a few decades earlier.

The Mississippian civilization had already left its mark by that time, in the form of sculptures and other artwork. A common set of symbols used in their religion, such as sunbursts, hands with eyes on them, crosses, and weeping eyes—some with potential connections to Mexican cultures—appears on tools, jewelry, and pottery throughout the region. This system of symbols, often referred to as the Southern Cult, shows the broad influence of the Mississippians and their religion.

Although the Mississippians were a warrior culture, they also made time for recreation. One game attributed to Mississippian tribes and played throughout the Southeast was called chunkey. A polished stone disc was rolled down a field, and players threw spears or poles at the place where they thought the stone would stop rolling. Whoever got his spear closest to the stone without actually hitting it won a point. Games were played until one person had twelve points. Almost every village had its own chunkey court, and people would bet heavily on the games.

Ancient art of the Mississippian culture influenced later indigenous people, such as Indians of the city of Natchez in present-day Mississippi. This face, probably of an ancient Mississippian warrior, is embossed in copper and was likely created around AD 1000. It is currently housed in the National Museum of the American Indian, Smithsonian Institution, in Washington, D.C.

The Cherokee

Another powerful southeastern tribe was the Cherokee. By 1492, they lived in about 200 large villages in present-day Tennessee, Virginia, and North Carolina. Their houses were constructed in a framework of woven branches and covered with mud. The Cherokee were farmers who had a government that allowed each village to remain independent. Still, the Cherokee worked together in times of war or other danger.

The Cherokee also had a highly developed social order. Roads connected their towns, and dugout canoes were used on the large rivers of their homeland. Although their later history was tragic (between 1838 and 1839 the U.S. Army forced the Cherokee out of their native lands on a migration known as the Trail of Tears, causing the death of thousands), Cherokee history is also

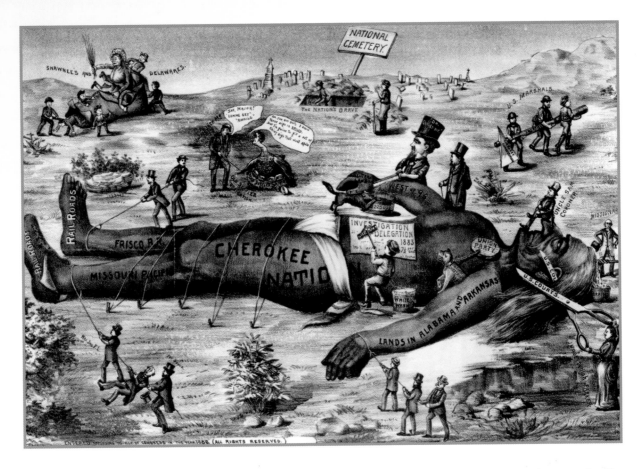

This 1886 historical caricature symbolizes the plight of the Cherokee Nation and the forced removal of its people due to the American hunger for land. The U.S. government made many false promises to the Cherokee in the form of treaties that were later broken, along with the threat of military force if they did not move from their native lands.

filled with great accomplishment. A Cherokee named Sequoyah was the first Native American to create an alphabet for his people; within a few years of his invention, most Cherokee could read and write. The Cherokee then created a written constitution for their people in the 1820s, and even during their exile in Oklahoma, they had their own newspapers and court system.

All the southeastern groups shared a belief that they were a people, not merely individual villages. Of all the groups in North America, these cultures came closest to having a true nation, like the countries of Europe at the same time. (Only the northeastern Iroquois and Huron tribes would come close to the level of organization of the southeastern groups.) For this reason, in the nineteenth century five of them (the Cherokee, Chickasaw, Choctaw, Creek, and Seminole) were called the Five Civilized Tribes.

Farther south, the Indians of Florida had developed their own ways of life in the subtropics. The Timucuan peoples were farmers who were influenced by the Mississippian people to their north. Timucuan tribes made villages with

Sequoyah *(left)*, a Cherokee scholar and tribal leader, created a written version of the Cherokee language. In this portrait, he is seen pointing to the syllabary he created, known as Talking Leaves, eighty-five letters that make up the Cherokee alphabet. A lithograph *(right)* illustrates the same Cherokee alphabet.

dome-shaped houses divided into several clans named after animals. Chiefs were chosen from the White Deer clan and were heavily tattooed and wore jewelry.

To the south of the Timucuans lived the Calusan peoples of southwest Florida. They were hunter-gatherers who built mounds for their temples. They hunted alligator and deer and caught fish, sharks, and rays. The Calusan also had a society based on separate classes, with a chief and his nobles, commoners, and slaves, who were mostly Indians from other tribes captured in battle.

Both the Timucuan and the Calusan had the misfortune of being located closest to the first Spanish colonies. Expeditions led by the Spanish beginning in the early 1500s—including Juan Ponce de León's fabled search for the fountain of youth—led to fighting between

The Spanish explorer Juan Ponce de León is seen searching for the fabled fountain of youth in this anonymous nineteenth-century painting. Because Europeans weren't sure of what to expect from the North American continent, many early books and works of art portrayed America as an unusual and mysterious land. Others illustrated the differences between America and Europe.

the Indians and the Europeans. These wars—and the infectious diseases such as smallpox, typhus, and influenza that soon engulfed all the indigenous peoples—destroyed Florida's original inhabitants by 1700.

At the time of Columbus, the northeastern section of the present-day United States was a vast expanse of forests. These dense woodlands stretched across the Appalachian Mountains and up into Maine and Canada. Yet this forest was not a wilderness; its Indian caretakers carefully tended it. Northeastern tribes had developed sophisticated farming techniques that utilized the land, providing the people with food and shelter. It was only after the invasion of the Europeans that the northeast evolved into an uninhabited wilderness, the impenetrable forest that greeted the early English colonists. When Captain John Smith, one of the first English colonists, visited present-day Massachusetts in 1614, for instance, he noted the land was "planted with gardens and corne fields" and

The eastern coast of North America from Virginia to New York is seen in this historic Dutch map from 1660. At the time, the Dutch had colonized a small portion of New England. In 1626, Dutch colonist and head of the Dutch West India Company Peter Minuit, "purchased" the island of Manhattan from local Native American tribes, renamed it New Amsterdam, and constructed a settlement there.

Indigenous Farming Methods

North American Indians reshaped the land according to their own needs and the needs of their animals. For instance, in order to create open grasslands suitable to feed game, they controlled underbrush by purposely burning large fields. In fact, Indians created much of the Midwestern prairie that exists today. Besides eating available plants, fruits, and nuts, Indian tribes successfully grew a variety of crops, including maize, squash, beans, and pumpkins. They did this by first dividing the land into small plots. Then they planted various interdependent crops (maize, squash, and beans were planted side by side, and the beans, which required support to grow, utilized the taller corn stalks for stability). Indians also practiced an early form of crop rotation. They abandoned farmlands after several years in order to eliminate the possibility of depleting the land's fertile resources.

Jacques Le Moyne, an artist who accompanied a French expedition to Florida in the 1560s, created this image of indigenous people of North America. He showed men and women and the differences in their farming practices. Men commonly used hoes made of animal bones to break up the ground, while women planted seeds. The clean lines in the soil drawn by Le Moyne, however, were common only in European farming at the time. This image was published in Theodor de Bry's *America*, a book illustrating scenes of America for a European audience.

"inhabited with a goodly, strong, and well-proportioned people."

The woodland tribes were also warriors, but the fiercest warriors of all had managed to unite in a democratic government. The region included Indians who survived as nomadic hunter-gatherers and those who settled villages united in powerful Indian nations.

Many different languages were spoken in the Northeast, but the most common language groups were Algonquian (also spelled Algonkian), which included dialects such as Delaware, Penobscot, and Iroquoian.

The Algonquian groups inhabited the coastal regions from Delaware to Maine. In the north, they survived by hunting and gathering plants. They also grew their own food, planting maize and other vegetables. Farther south, the longer summer season allowed farming to become much more important than hunting had been. Tending the land for a greater portion of the year also encouraged more permanent settlements and higher populations. These tribes were becoming nations in more ways than the northern tribes in Maine or Vermont.

The Iroquois

The Iroquois were farmers who primarily relied on harvested crops for most of their food. Because of this, they lived in settled villages, each protected with a high palisade, or wall built of sharpened tree trunks planted in the ground. Although the Iroquois were not nomads like the northern Algonquian groups, they relocated their villages when local

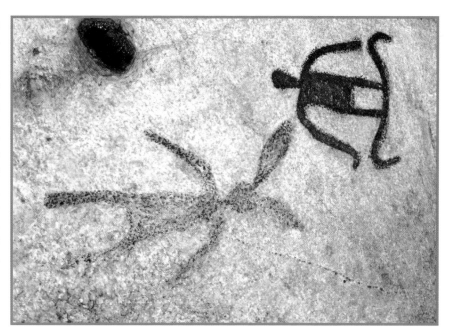

This Algonquian petroglyph of two figures was cut into a rock in Ontario, Canada. Algonquian-speaking tribes were a related band of hunters and trappers who lived in the northern United States and Canada. They traveled great distances by canoe for the purposes of trade and capturing small animals. All of the Algonquian tribes shared a common language and the same creation myths and religious beliefs.

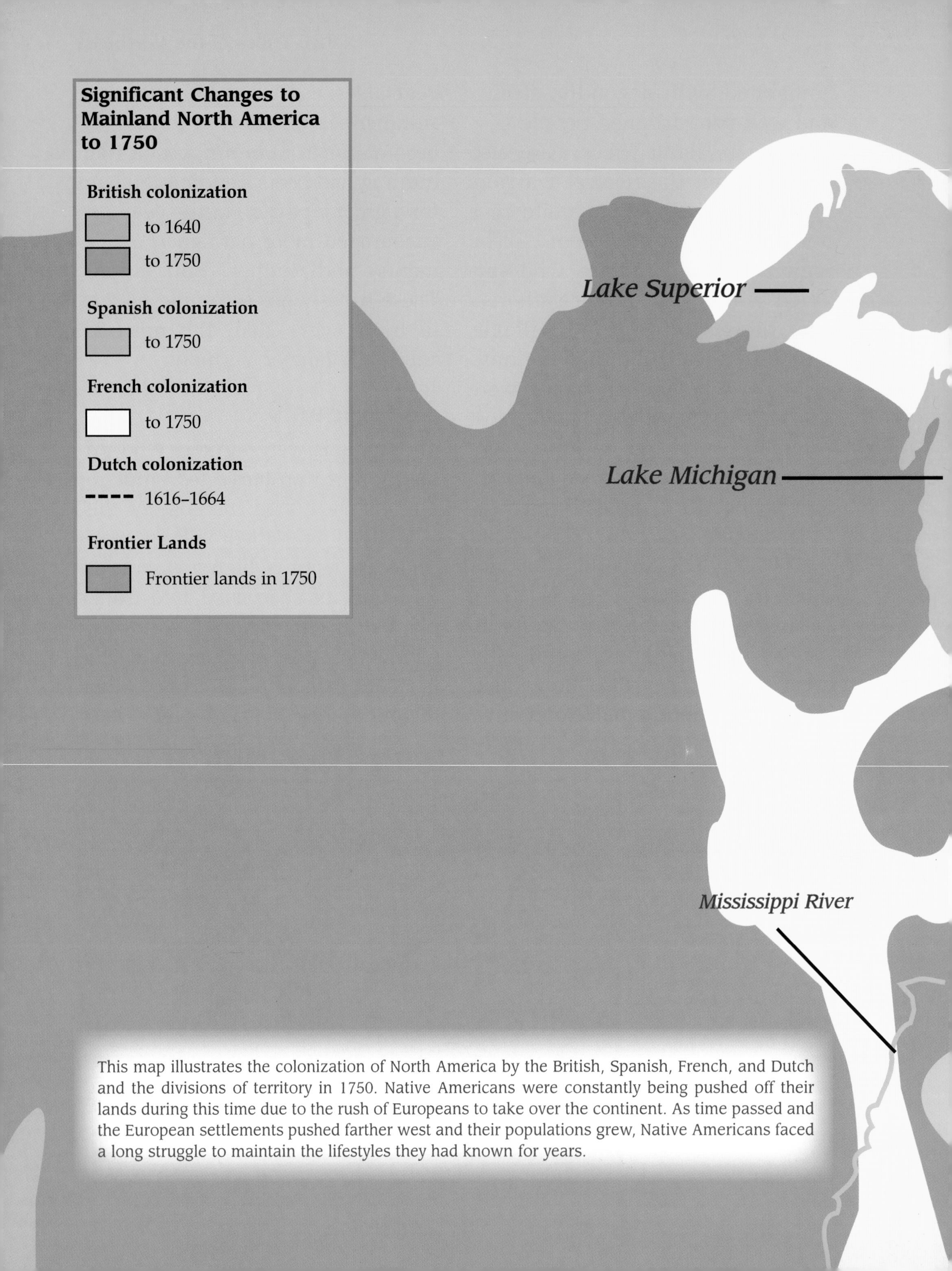

Lake Superior ——

Lake Michigan ——————

Mississippi River

This map illustrates the colonization of North America by the British, Spanish, French, and Dutch and the divisions of territory in 1750. Native Americans were constantly being pushed off their lands during this time due to the rush of Europeans to take over the continent. As time passed and the European settlements pushed farther west and their populations grew, Native Americans faced a long struggle to maintain the lifestyles they had known for years.

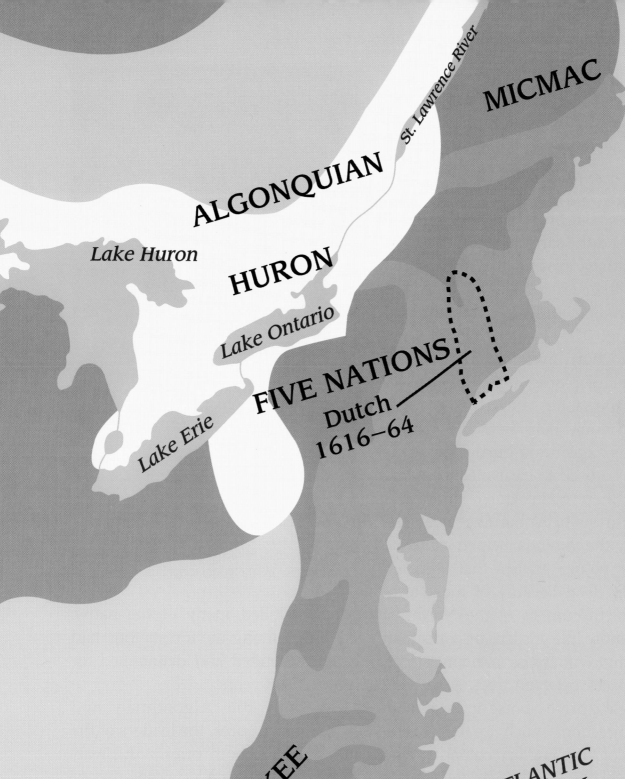

MICMAC

ALGONQUIAN

St. Lawrence River

Lake Huron

HURON

Lake Ontario

FIVE NATIONS

Lake Erie

Dutch
1616–64

CHEROKEE

ATLANTIC
OCEAN

areas had run out of animals to hunt or the soil was no longer able to grow enough food. Usually this happened about every ten to fifty years.

Both groups grew the "three sisters" of North American farming: corn, squash, and beans. Both groups also used the same technique to clear away the forest so that they could grow their crops. This method was known as swidden, or slashing and burning. The Indians would light fires to burn away the underbrush and small plants, then use hoes to rake the ashes into the ground, which would help the plants grow.

This slash-and-burn technique was also used to clear meadows that deer—their main source of meat—liked to visit; by burning away the brush, the Indians helped cultivate tender young grasses that attracted hungry deer. Because of these techniques, the forests of the Northeast were more like gardens or parks than unkempt wilderness; in many places, the spaces between trees were wide enough to drive a horse and wagon in any direction, much to the amazement of the English colonists who arrived later. But the war and disease the Europeans brought to North

The Iroquois man in this illustration is fishing from a canoe. Iroquois tribes were divided into clans with distinct rules about classes and marriage rites. They were excellent farmers and hunters and lived close together in traditional longhouses.

America killed many of the native peoples, ruining the forests they had carefully tended and maintained for hundreds of years.

In both the Algonquian and Iroquoian cultures, the leaders of the villages were both priests and warriors. They were called powwows or sachems, and they were considered

The historic map on the opposite page shows the approximate placement of Iroquois and Algonquian tribes around 1650. The Iroquois were an alliance of Native American tribes (Cayuga, Mohawk, Oneida, Onondaga, and Seneca) known as the League of Five Nations. Because the government of the Five Nations was so similar to a basic democracy, the founding fathers of the United States looked to it as a model during the writing of the Constitution.

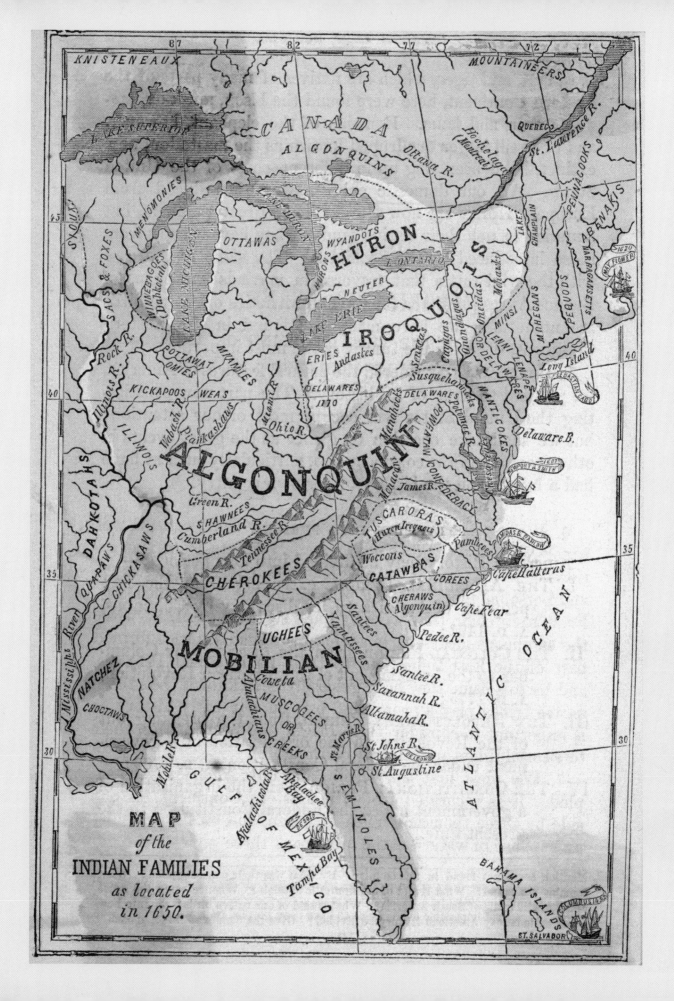

MAP
of the
INDIAN FAMILIES
as located
in 1650.

to have magical and spiritual powers in addition to being leaders. However, as leaders, they listened to the needs of their tribes. Most decisions were made according to the desires of the group.

One of the finest crafts produced by the tribes of the Northeast was the making of wampum. Wampum consisted of beads made from the shells of clams, especially those with purple shells. Contrary to popular belief, wampum was not used as money before the arrival of the Europeans but as a diplomatic offering. Because the beads were hard to make and the shells difficult to find, they were important trade items throughout the region. The Quohog people of present-day Rhode Island were experts in the making of wampum.

The Iroquoian-speaking groups were a strong and competitive people and frequently fought among themselves. They lived in villages of as many as 2,000 people, in large longhouses made of logs and bark. Each longhouse was up to 200 feet (61 m) long and provided shelter for several related families.

The Five Nations

Around the time of Columbus's first voyage to the Americas, the Iroquois had organized themselves into large groups, or confederations, of tribes. Members of a confederation agreed to avoid infighting and to defend each other in case of attack by outside tribes. The two largest confederations were the Huron, or Wendat, confederation in what is now Ontario, Canada, and the League of Five Nations, or Haudenosaunee (People of the Longhouse) in northern New York State. The Huron were the larger of the two confederations but were destroyed by disease and conflict with Europeans, mostly French colonists in Canada in the early 1600s. The Iroquois confederation still exists today.

One of the most remarkable facts about the League of Five Nations is that it was essentially a democracy

This purple wampum belt was found in northeastern North America and is attributed to Algonquian tribes. The bead designs and colors of the belt denote agreements and events important in politics, history, and religion. The design of the three rectangles suggests an alliance of three groups in war.

that later influenced the framers of the U.S. Constitution. Sachems from each of the tribes—the Seneca, Cayuga, Onondaga, Oneida, and Mohawk—met in a council of fifty men. The council helped keep the peace among the nations, making sure that none of them felt wronged by another. The council also organized the wars the Iroquois fought against other tribes in the region. The council did not interfere in the daily activities of each of its tribes. In many ways, it was an ideal balance between the common good of the Five Nations and individual freedom for all the Haudenosaunee. It was for this reason that the Five Nations were studied by the authors of the U.S. Constitution.

Conclusion

No one is sure how many people lived in North America before the coming of the Europeans. It is a controversial topic. If there were few people living in America, then the occupation of the continent by the Europeans would not seem so bad. They would have been taking unused land, not forcing people off the land they had lived on for years.

For most of the twentieth century, it was thought that only about 1 million people lived in America north of Mexico in 1492. Today, that number is seen as being far too small. There

A Mohawk is seen in this eighteenth-century watercolor. The Mohawk peoples had nine representatives in the League of Five Nations. They lived primarily in the eastern woodlands of North America.

were probably at least 8.5 million people in North America alone, and that number may have been as high as 15 million. Mexico, with its centuries of steady farming and large

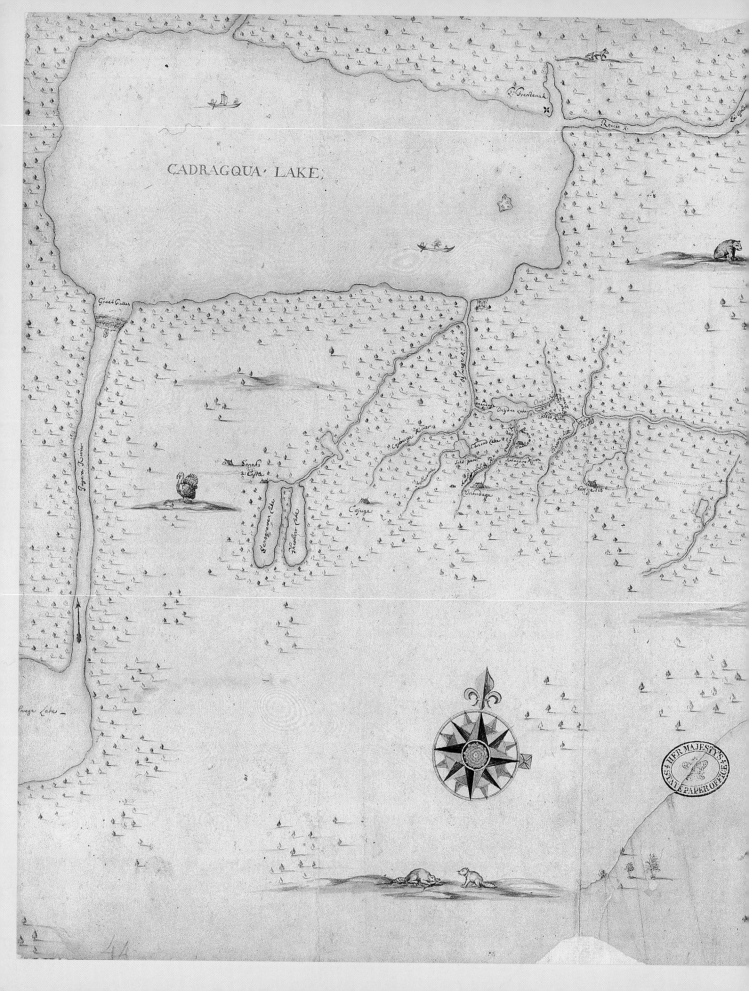

CADRAGQUA· LAKE:

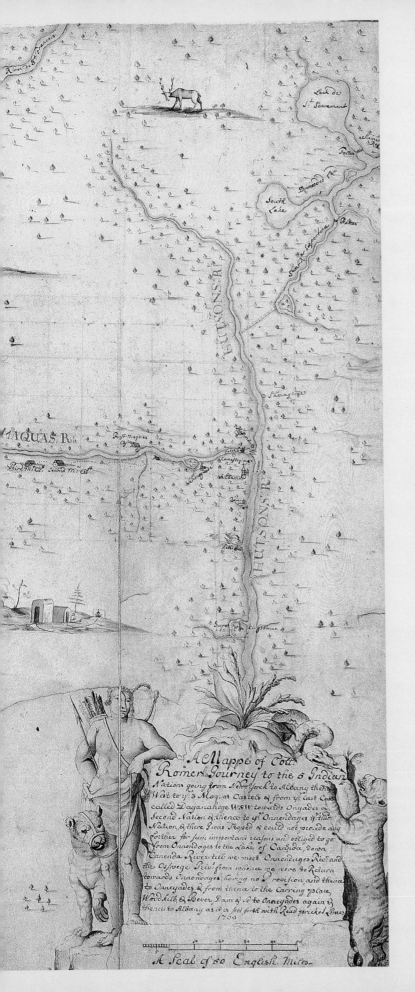

A map showing Romer's journey to the Five Nations going from New York to Albany. This historic map was created in 1700 by French explorers who were scouting the area between New York and the Great Lakes region. At the time, this territory was controlled by Iroquois tribes who were often at war with advancing French, Dutch, and British explorers, each seeking territory to colonize in the eastern United States.

A detail of a winter "count," a Native American pictorial record that was passed from one generation to another and recounted major events that took place each year. Native Americans often kept records of famines, buffalo hunts, severe storms, smallpox epidemics, and other significant events. The arrival of Christopher Columbus is noted on one winter count, as was the introduction of horses to Native American tribes.

cities, supported millions more. All these populations were drastically reduced by the European invasion.

Diseases did most of the killing. Illnesses like smallpox, measles, and syphilis had never been known in America, and the native peoples had no resistance to them. Death rates for some of these diseases may have been 90 percent or higher. Whole nations vanished from Earth in a matter of only a few years.

Those that did not die of disease often died in wars with the Europeans. The military advantages of the invaders, especially because of their horses and guns, usually allowed them to defeat much larger forces. Hernán Cortés conquered the Aztecs without ever having more than a thousand Spaniards in Mexico; the Pequot Nation, some of the fiercest warriors in New England, were eliminated by several hundred Englishmen. In the early days of the conquest, the Europeans were often aided by the native peoples themselves. Native Americans saw the coming of the invaders as a chance to defeat their own enemies, never dreaming that their "allies" would turn on them.

Despite all this, the Indians of the Americas have left their stamp on world history. Two of the four basic crops grown for food in the world today (corn and potatoes) are directly from the Americas. Tomatoes, chocolate, and tobacco can also be attributed to North America. The immense store of knowledge of herbs and plants accumulated by the Indians is another way in which they have made their mark. More than 500 drugs used today were originally used by these native peoples.

In 1492, the peoples of North America lived well by forming a balanced relationship with the land. They followed long-established traditions that had served them for centuries. Great civilizations had risen and fallen, and new civilizations were beginning to rise. But all this would be swept away by the waves of European colonists. The story of how these Europeans, and the Africans they brought with them, transformed a continent is referred to as the Columbian Exchange.

TIMELINE

18,000–12,000 BC Paleo-Indians cross the glacial land bridge later known as Beringia that was once situated between Alaska and Russia.

10,000 BC Glacial ice melts in North America.

4000 BC The first small mounds are built by early Mississippian cultures.

1500 BC The Olmecs build the first cities in the Americas.

1200 BC Maize and techniques for its cultivation are introduced to the Southwest from Mexico.

200 BC The Hopewell culture emerges in the eastern United States and its people build mounds in the Ohio River valley.

AD 400 Hopewell mound building ceases.

500 The Hopewell culture begins its decline. Anasazi settlements are established in Mesa Verde, Colorado. The bow and arrow is in use in the Great Plains.

800 Maize and beans are cultivated in North America.

950 Effigy mounds begin appearing throughout the Midwest.

1000 Vikings establish settlements in Newfoundland. Pottery is made throughout the eastern United States.

1100 The height of the Mississippian culture; Cahokia, one of its largest towns, is a center of trade and commerce.

1200 Cahokia begins its decline. Beans are a staple crop of the people of the eastern woodlands.

1250 The Anasazi begin abandoning large group dwellings and move south to forts on hilltops.

1272–1299 A period marked by drought in North America.

1300 Cahokia is abandoned. The Anasazi civilization completely collapses.

1348 The Black Death rages throughout Europe.

1350 The cultures of the Southern Cult reach their peak of influence.

1400 The European Renaissance begins.

1450 The Iroquois found the League of Five Nations.

1492 Christopher Columbus lands on an island in the Bahamas he names San Salvador. Europeans and North Americans have permanent contact for the first time.

GLOSSARY

Anasazi The ancient civilization of the American Southwest. The word "Anasazi" is a Pueblo word meaning "ancient outsider." The Anasazi had an advanced civilization that collapsed in the 1300s.

chunkey Popular game of the southeastern Native American peoples.

counting coup Plains peoples' practice of touching an enemy, alive or dead, during combat.

dugout canoe Large canoe made out of a tree, hollowed out by fires, and then carved into a boat.

Five Civilized Tribes Nineteenth-century term for the Cherokee, Chickasaw, Choctaw, Creek, and Seminole peoples, originally from the southeastern part of the United States. These people had strong tribes with central leadership and were close to being nations similar to the European countries.

Great Basin The arid region of the Rocky Mountains centered in present-day Utah and Nevada.

hogan Eight-sided Navajo house made of wood covered with bark and earth.

kachina Hopi spirits and gods, often represented by small dolls.

kiva The basement of a pueblo building, where only men were allowed; used for sacred rites and as a gathering place.

medicine wheels Large stone circles found in the northern Great Plains; they may have been burial sites or ancient astronomical observatories.

mound builders The cultures of the Ohio River valley such as the Adena and Hopewell, who built enormous earth mounds, often in the shape of animals or symbols.

Plateau The high region of the Rocky Mountains in the northwestern United States.

powwow A leader of the eastern woodlands people, especially those who lived in New England and Long Island; also, a gathering of a tribe or tribes for ceremonies and dancing.

pueblo The apartment-like buildings of the southwestern native peoples.

sachem The leader of the Iroquois and other eastern tribes; he was both priest and ruler.

Southern Cult The symbolic language of the southeastern peoples, which shows a heavy Mexican influence; the symbols used in this religion were also used by peoples throughout the Southeast.

Sun Dance A ritual of the people of the Plains in which young men were hung from cords that were sewn into their shoulders, chest, and legs; surviving this agony gave the young men honor.

tepee A shelter of the people of the Plains made up of hides stretched over a frame of wooden poles.

totem pole A tall wooden pole carved with the faces of animals and spirits, made by the northwestern peoples.

wampum Beads made of the shells of clams, used as a sign of peace treaties and a trade good by the eastern woodlands peoples.

wickiup Shelter used by the Great Basin peoples made of bundles of brush tied together.

FOR MORE INFORMATION

Institute of American Indian
　Arts (IAIA)
83 Avan Nu Po Road
Santa Fe, NM 87505
(505) 424-2300
Web site: http://www.iaiancad.org

Web Sites

Due to the changing nature of Internet links, the Rosen Publishing Group, Inc., has developed an online list of Web sites related to the subject of this book. This site is updated regularly. Please use this link to access the list:

http://www.rosenlinks.com/ushagn/nabc

FOR FURTHER READING

Grinde, Donald, and Bruce Johansen. *Encyclopedia of Native American Biography.* New York: Henry Holt & Co., 1997.

Hakim, Joy. *The First Americans.* New York: Oxford University Press, 2003.

Josephy, Alvin M., Jr., ed. *America in 1492.* New York: Vintage Books, 1991.

Juettner, Bonnie. *100 Native Americans Who Shaped American History.* San Mateo, CA: Bluewood Books, 2002.

Porter, Frank III, ed. *Native American Religion.* Broomall, PA: Chelsea House, 1995.

Pritzker, Barry M. *Native American Encyclopedia: History, Culture, and Peoples.* New York: Oxford University Press, 2000.

BIBLIOGRAPHY

Barker, Alex W. "Myths and Monsters: Decoding Ritual Images of a Mysterious Ancient American Religion." *Archaeology* 55 (July/ August 2002): pp. 40–45.

Begley, Sharon. "The First Americans." *Newsweek* (Fall/Winter 1991): pp. 15–20.

Hoxie, Frederick E. (Editor). *Encyclopedia of North American Indians: Native American History,* *Culture, and Life from Paleo-Indians to the Present.* New York: Houghton-Mifflin Co., 1996.

Josephy, Alvin M. *500 Nations: An Illustrated History of North American Indians.* New York: Gramercy, 2002.

Lovgren, Stefan. "Who Were the First Americans?" Nationalgeographic. com. Retrieved October 15, 2003. (http://news.nationalgeographic. com/news/2003/09/0903_030903 _bajaskull.html).

Mann, Charles C. "1491." *The Atlantic Monthly* 289 (March 2002): pp. 41–53.

Miller, Donald L. "A Biography of America: New World Encounters." Learner.org. Retrieved October 19, 2003. (http://www.learner.org/biographyofamerica/prog01/transcript/page02.html).

"Mystery of the First Americans." PBS.org. Retrieved October 15, 2003. (http://www.pbs.org/wgbh/nova/transcrips/2705first.html).

Zinn, Howard. A *People's History of the United States: 1492–Present*. New York: Harper Perennial, 2003.

INDEX

About the Author

Fred Ramen is a writer and computer programmer who is the author of thirteen books for Rosen Publishing, including biographies of Hernán Cortés and Joe Montana. His interests include military history, science fiction, and French cuisine. Mr. Ramen lives in New York City with his wife, Allison, and cat, Sweetie.

Photo Credits

Cover background, pp. 1, 40–41 © Library of Congress, Geography and Map Division; cover (top right), pp. 44 (left) © Library of Congress; cover (bottom right), pp. 36, 37 © Historical Picture Archive/Corbis; p. 4–5 © Maps.com/Corbis; p. 6 © The Art Archive/Naval Museum Madrid/ Dagli Orti; pp. 7, 17 © Tom Bean/Corbis; pp. 8–9, 12–13, 32, 34–35, 50–51 Maps designed by Tahara Hasan; p. 10 © Archivo Iconografico S.A./Corbis; p. 14 © Richard A. Cooke/Corbis; p. 15 © Raymond Gehman/Corbis; p. 16 © Michael S. Lewis/Corbis; pp. 18, 21 © Werner Forman; p. 20 © Craig Aurness/Corbis; p. 22 © Canadian Museum of Civilization/Corbis; p. 23 © Museum of History and Industry/Corbis; pp. 24–25, 30–31 courtesy of the General Libraries, the University of Texas at Austin; pp. 26, 53 © Bettmann/Corbis; p. 31 (right) © Buddy Mays/ Corbis; p. 38 © Northwestern University Library, Edward S. Curtis's *The North American Indian: The Photographic Images,* 2001; p. 39 © Western History/Genealogy Department, Denver Public Library; p. 42 © Werner Forman/Art Resource, New York; p. 43 © Library of Congress, Prints and Photographs Division; p. 44 (right) © Corbis; p. 45 © The New York Public Library, Art Resource, New York; pp. 46–47 © The Art Archive/John Webb; p. 48 © The Art Archive/New York Public Library/HarperCollins Publishers; p. 49 © Robert Estall/Corbis; p. 52 © Mary Evans Picture Library; p. 54 © HIP/Scala/Art Resource, New York; p. 55 © The Art Archive/Musée de Nouveau Monde La Rochelle/Dagli Orti; pp. 56–57 © The Art Archive/Public Records Office London/HarperCollins Publishers; p. 58 © Library of Congress, Manuscript Division.

Designer: Tahara Hasan; **Editor:** Joann Jovinelly